"If you long to embrace God's forgiveness so you can move forward without fear into His glorious freedom, read this book. Lynn Neely's story of overcoming guilt, shame, and brokenness will give you the blueprint to do the same. You'll find hope, truth, and practical steps for a productive and meaningful life in each chapter."

Carol Kent, Executive Director of Speak Up Ministries, Speaker and Author, *He Holds My Hand: Experiencing God's Presence & Protection* (Tyndale)

"Heartfelt and courageous, *Hope on a Mission: Forgiveness and Healing* is a powerful testimony of grace and self-forgiveness. With raw honesty, the author takes us on her journey through torturous decisions and regrets, and leads us to a place of forgiveness and peace."

Robyn Dykstra, Speaker, Author, and Speaking Coach

"It is with great joy that I endorse the book, *Hope on a Mission: Forgiveness and Healing* by Lynn Neely. I have been Lynn's pastor for many years. She is a mature follower of Jesus, who has transformed her life for His glory. Her testimony is one of redemption and forgiveness. You will be amazed as you read about what God has done. It will be a blessing to you."

Dr. Terry Jacobs, Adjunct Professor with Lancaster Bible College and pastor of the Seneca Evangelical Church

"With so many super sensitive issues confronting Christians in our modern day, it is refreshing to read of the testimonies of individuals that have faced life struggles and have come through them with victory. Jesus promised 'power to be a witness' in Acts 1:8. Lynn, in this book, opens herself to the power offered by Jesus, so healing can come to others in a beautiful way."

Reverend Richard L. Weagraff,
President, P.U.M.P. Ministries Inc.

HOPE ON A MISSION

Forgiveness and Healing

Lynn Neely

EABooks Publishing
Your Partner In Publishing

ISBN: 978-1-963611-90-8
LCCN: 2024926612

Cover design: Robin Black
Cover photo: iStock-viktoriaa

Published by EA Books Publishing, a division of Living Parables of Central Florida, Inc. a 501c3

EABooksPublishing.com

FOREWORD

The gifting and passion the Spirit of God placed in my heart after my salvation in 1974 has been to tell and teach about the life-changing power of the Living God through Bible studies at churches and in homes, jail ministry, mentoring, and song.

I first met the author (I call her Lynn!) in 1991 when a new church was being planted in our area of small towns. She was part of the phone ministry, calling area people and telling them of a great new vacation Bible school that was going to be held in our county park that summer and explaining that a new church was coming to town!

That VBS would be the start of a church that continues faithfully today. I arrived on the scene when the church purchased a small out-of-business fitness center as their building. It was a church plant, and I wasn't interested, and yet the Lord led me there through a series of undeniable circumstances, instruction from His Word, and through His Spirit. He told me that I was being sent there to be a teacher.

When I first met Lynn, I sensed a kindred spirit and immediately recognized that we had similar traits, which I instinctively (supernaturally) knew had their source from childhood abuse, family dysfunction, and addiction. Some healing and God-love and lessons I had received, that she had not yet experienced, drew me to her even more than her vivacious personality and sincere love for people. She was lovingly known as "Mary Sunshine" for her cheery outlook and quick laughter, but her deepest secret and shame had not yet been revealed and healed by our Lord Jesus.

Lynn sees a person's need and desires to meet it. It is a God-given gift and desire. It is this God-gift that prompted her to publish her hopeful and riveting testimony in the anthology book *Anchor in the Storm, Vol. 2.*

In this project, *Hope on a Mission: Forgiveness and Healing,* she adds to her testimony the God-stories of others she has met along the way. Page after page is heart-wrenching, heartwarming, sometimes bringing me to tears, sometimes renewing my hope.

I can sum up Lynn's heart and passion in her own words:

From Chapter 1, p. 9, "God has placed on my heart the large number of pews filled with many, many people like myself . . . saved . . . forgiven . . . yet *not healed.* Maybe they haven't been able to believe or accept God's forgiveness and are repeatedly asking God to forgive them in case they forgot, or He did not hear them the first time, just as I did for years."

In Chapter 4, p. 41, "I not only had to trust God to be strong and courageous to stand up and share my testimony but also to bring it into the light, out of the darkness, so I finally could be convinced of my forgiveness and freedom. Christians need to do this to spread God's light into the darkness in our world."

And finally, p. 54, "God doesn't just want to save us for a future with Him but He wants to set us free here and now!"

In this book Lynn shares her heart, and the heart of God for *you*. I couldn't put it down.

—Diane C. Webb
September 2024

CONTENTS

ACKNOWLEDGEMENTS

First of all, I would like to thank God for sending His Son, Jesus, who died for my sins on the cross, rose again, rejoined His Father in heaven, and who has been and is with me, always, and has counted the number of hairs on my head even before I was born.

I would like also to thank Him for giving me this assignment and for seeing it to completion. He has worked all things for good in my life, as He has promised, because I love Him. I pray that this book gives His hope to all of the brokenhearted that He plans to reach by putting it into their hands, minds, and hearts. I give Him all the glory.

I am grateful for all of my family and want to thank Denny, Casey, Meg, Buck, and Brie for giving me their permission to share all of our stories to give so many others hope. I would like to thank you, especially, Denny, for putting up with me for almost a half of a century now, and for having patience with me through this process of speaking, writing, and publishing the book that God assigned me to complete for Him.

I know it hasn't always been easy. You still have the prettiest eyes and eyelashes that I have ever seen. You are the best and make life fun! I love and appreciate you so much for standing by me all of these years. Thank you!

I want to express my gratitude to all those who have prayed for me and invested heart, energy, time, and finances into any part of my life, including for the Continental Ministry trip. There are too many of you to mention, but God knows who you are. I pray God's abundant blessings will be poured out on you.

I would also like to thank many other precious friends and acquaintances who God put into my life for their permission to share their stories, including testimonies from the Encore Continental Ministry group, to show God's hope and love.

I especially want to thank my small group of prayer warriors—Diane, Karen, Lori, and Annette—who have my and each other's back in prayer and every other way through thick and thin, no matter what. This group includes Diane, who wrote the forward for my book with very short notice, who also has been my Christian mentor for many years. I don't know where I would be without your speaking God's Word into my life just when I need it! Thank you! And, thank you, Karen and Diane, for all the unforgettable worship team memories!

And Jen, how can I thank you enough for all of the encouragement through the years since I first told you that God told me to write a book and for the long hours of editing. I appreciate your help and support so much! Thank you!

There would not be any pictures in this book without your help, Pat. Thank you for making the pictures possible for inclusion. What would I do without you?

I want to thank all those who gave their beautiful endorsements for this book. You all mean the world to me!

And Cheri Cowell, Rebecca Ford, Robin Black, Monica Miller, and the rest of your team at EAPublishing, I wish to thank you for all of the work and prayer you put into your books and for making this book possible. Cheri, I guess our Lord knew what His plan was seven years ago, when we met on the phone before I went to my first Speak Up Conference in Grand Rapids, Michigan, where He kept throwing us together the whole conference. He really does have quite the sense of humor and works in mysterious ways!

Thank you to any others that I may have forgotten to include; God sees you.

God bless you all, and to God be the glory!

DEDICATION

I would like to dedicate this book in memory of Mike, a nice young man who played the saxophone in our Encore Continental Singing Ministries orchestra during our 2009 mission trip to the United Kingdom (UK).

I was first introduced to Mike, approximately 25 years old, during our week of rehearsal camp in Enniskillen, Northern Ireland, at the Clinton Center Hostel. He told me that he had gone on a couple of other mission trips with the Continental Ministries in the past, which I thought was terrific for him to raise sponsorship money several times since he was such a young man.

As our three-week missionary trip evolved with our daily schedules, I got to know the director and his family, the two assistant directors, and the chorus and orchestra participants a little better, including Mike. He seemed very quiet and shy, usually keeping to himself. During our mealtimes, the ladies around my age would often sit with the bus driver, Alan, and his wife, June. They were great and were just a bit older than we were.

It seemed odd to me that Mike would always enjoy his meals sitting at our table with our group of older ladies instead of with some of the other younger guys who were more his age. So, one night I asked one of the younger guys closer to Mike's age if he would come over and invite Mike to join them at their table. He said he would, and a few minutes later, he did just that. Mike graciously told him that he was fine where he was. He remained seated with us, "old ladies," as I called us, which was fine.

Mike seemed to be where I was often, almost like he was drawn to me, whether we would bump into each other in the hall unexpectedly in the down times of our schedule where he would just be hanging out by himself or at other similar such times. I would usually talk to him in passing for a few moments about where some of the different people in our tour group were off to during that time slot. I would mention that he should have gone along, and he would reply that they asked him to go but that he wanted to stay at the hostel.

My Christian mentor friend told me that people may sometimes be drawn to us and not know precisely why themselves, but it is Christ in us to whom they are drawn. I figured it was either that or maybe I was like a mother figure to him. God knows. Either way, although odd, I was okay with it.

After we returned from our trip, I was in touch with a lady via e-mail from California who had been on the tour with us. In April of the following year, I got an unexpected e-mail from her explaining to me that Mike had been working for a logging company in Maryland near his home, had suffered a heat stroke, was hospitalized, unable to respond, was not doing well at all, and needed our prayers. I live in Pennsylvania, and it was unseasonably hot early that year. I began to pray for Mike and his family, as many others did, including those on tour with him. Mike's mom started a page for him on Caring Bridge to keep friends and family updated on his condition as we continued lifting him in our prayers.

Mike battled for his young life here on earth for quite a long while, but sadly, we received the news that God took him home to be with Him. I was shocked and heartbroken for his family and immediately started lifting them in prayer for strength and comfort, and that God would give them hope.

Mike was a gentle young man taken so early in his life, yet I am thankful that he knew Jesus as his personal Lord and Savior and is in heaven with Him. Not everyone, especially young, can say they have made that critical life choice. I am also happy that I had the privilege of meeting and getting to know him and that God shared him with me and others while he was here. And am so thankful that he was obedient to share Jesus's light, salt, and the gospel of hope to so many others through his smile and musical talent more than once, even halfway around the world.

TO THE READER

The reason I am writing this book is, first and foremost, because God told me to do so. The second purpose for this book to be written is because it is my prayer that no woman of any age will make the same wrong decision I made in my young life for any reason.

I also pray that by reading this book, those who have made a bad choice that they regret will find forgiveness and make peace with their past. I want all women and men to heal from the brokenness in their lives so they can minister to future generations.

The third reason for this book is because I want everyone to know that there is forgiveness, healing, and hope for us all that comes from God's mercy and grace. The story of the gospel is simple. God offers His gift of salvation to all people who confess their sin, turn away from it, and ask Jesus Christ into their hearts to become their personal Lord and Savior.

The Holy Spirit then lives inside you to help provide His truth and guidance as you live out your life (it is also important to tell someone that you have accepted Jesus into your heart as your Savior). Then, find a

Bible-believing church to attend and a Christian friend who can help disciple you as you read the Bible, pray, and become more spiritually mature.

I would like to share a few testimony stories throughout this book, some of which were shared halfway around the world while I had the privilege of being on an Encore Continental Ministries Singing Mission tour, to show you God's hope and just how great God's love is for us.

The world needs to know that Jesus loves them and has the power to change their brokenness into wholeness. Music transcends every language and cultural barrier, and those of us who know Jesus as Savior certainly have something to sing about! The Continentals began more than forty years ago as a non-profit organization that gave those with a passion for Jesus Christ, music, and the performing arts an opportunity to share the Gospel of Jesus Christ in this powerful way.

The Continentals had two singing groups, some with orchestras, that toured at that time and over the years. One group was younger, approximately ages 16 years to age 21 years, and the other group was ages 21 years and older. The group with older individuals was called the Encore Continental Ministries. There were about 25 singers, as well as a small orchestra, a technical team, two assistant directors and a director and his family who happened to be from England, in our group. We attended a one-week long rehearsal camp in Enniskillen, Ireland and then traveled by bus throughout southern

Ireland, England, Scotland, and Wales. We stayed with host families as we sang in churches, cathedrals, and schools. We stayed in a hostel if there were not enough host families. We each raised our own sponsorship money for the awesome opportunity to go spread the Gospel with the Continentals, which not only covered our expenses but also was used so that everyone who wanted to do so could attend our concerts free of charge. Sadly, I recently found out that the Continentals no longer exist in the United States at this time. It is my understanding that they still spread the Gospel in the UK. It truly was an opportunity of a lifetime!

HOPE ON A MISSION

Forgiveness and Healing

Introduction

The number one elective medical procedure in the US is abortion. Staggering, right? How is that possible?

Well, when you're young and scared and the shame of an unplanned pregnancy feels so heavy you can't breathe, abortion can feel like the only viable option. When you feel trapped, but you're terrified to ask your parents for help for fear of their reaction, abortion can feel like your only solution. At least, that's what it felt like for me.

I got pregnant when I was 19. My boyfriend and I had been dating for a couple of years. We had been abstinent, but it only took one weak moment. I knew if I told my mother, she'd kill me. I knew it. So, instead of telling her, I told a friend, who then told me that she'd had two abortions. She said she would take me to the clinic.

When I told my boyfriend my decision, he was not for it, but said he would support me no matter what I decided.

He told me he would marry me, but then I'd still have to tell my mother about the pregnancy, and I could not!

I did my best to love and honor both of my parents. I wanted their approval and thought it would help keep the peace at home.

After I graduated from high school, I attended school in the inner city, two hours from my home, while still dating my high school sweetheart, whom I had started dating in my senior year. I completed my training and returned home to pursue a career as a medical laboratory assistant, while my boyfriend stayed in the city after completing his schooling to work a new job in the suburbs.

I'd worked hard to create a new life affirming my mother's pride. I thought I couldn't start over with a baby. I panicked with fear . . . I felt trapped. That's why I decided to have an abortion, but I can tell you now I made a wrong decision.

I remember standing at the desk of the abortion clinic across from the nurse with black hair, filling out paperwork, wondering how I got to this point. On the inside, I was so worried about having unhealthy future pregnancies, internal bleeding, and infertility, but I had no one to talk to about it.

I didn't want to have an abortion. I wished I could be anywhere else but in that clinic. I was scared to my core. I can still hear the oldies song that was playing on the radio. After the "procedure," I asked to see the aborted remains. That memory will always be with me. I left the clinic as quickly as I was able and stuffed all the shame and guilt as far down as it would go.

Then, I went on as if life was usual.

Janet's Story

Janet said she was raised in a Christian family, but her parents were abusive. Nothing filled that hole in her heart, and she was searching for hope and love, which she looked for in many different ways.

While in high school, after becoming prom queen, she discovered that she was successful at being famous. But that didn't even fill that hole in her heart; she said it almost made it worse.

Then she tried an eating disorder to fill the void, but starving herself just made it worse. She thought if she tried busyness in college and got involved in many things, she would feel love and have hope. It didn't work.

The hole remained and the striving to fill it grew more. She tried relationships and thought the right guy might help her feel loved, but that didn't work either.

She felt like she had nothing. No hope. She cried to God, "If you are there, you must show me something."

A couple of days later, somebody came into her life and showed her love in a way she had never seen before. She asked them why they loved her so much. Why did they care about her? They said they cared because Christ loved them and that Christ loved her. That was a different love than she knew.

She got curious and started reading the Bible. The God of the Bible was a lot different than she had thought all those years; He was loving and passionate to His people. That's what she wanted! *That* love.

That space in her heart where He was supposed to be was filled with so many different things that God couldn't fit in. Something had to be cleaned out but she knew she couldn't do it in her power.

She kept reading about Jesus and how He came to earth and lived a perfect, sinless life. He died on the cross, took all of her sin and shame, and put it on Himself. That's when she asked Jesus into her heart and told Him she seriously needed Him, His love, and His cleansing because her heart was filled with nasty things. And He did. She said He came into her life and gave her a love like none other she's ever known, like nothing anybody or anything could give her. He brought the hope that she had never experienced. It was indescribable.

Janet said at times she still wonders, *God, are you still there?* But in those moments when she is insecure and doubting, He whispers in her heart, *Yeah, I'm still here, and I still love you.* She ended her testimony story by saying, "If you are in a place where you don't know where to turn, or you feel hopeless, I understand, but God understands more. There is hope; it's found in Jesus Christ."

CHAPTER 1

GUILT/SHAME/ BROKENNESS

The intense guilt and shame I felt from making an irreversible, wrong decision and keeping it in the darkness for years kept brewing, causing excruciatingly painful and inadequate feelings deep down inside my inner being.

When you're in this situation, you can do nothing to change that terrible past decision in your life. *Ever!* Carrying this burden is unbelievably hard.

According to the Cambridge Dictionary, brokenness is "a state of strong emotional pain that stops someone from living a normal or healthy life."

The Merriam-Webster definition includes "not functioning; damaged, weakened in strength; crushed by bad experiences."

I had a deep, dark, dirty secret that had been buried for so many years that even though I didn't think of it constantly, it colored every choice I made and every attitude I had toward myself and others. I often wondered what people would think—friends, relatives, co-workers, bosses—if they knew my secret.

I was often very tentative about making decisions and had a low self-esteem. And no wonder! After all, what kind of person decides to abort her child? Abortion stops a beating heart! Even after all those years, I couldn't believe I could do such a thing.

Have you ever seen the cartoon picture where a person is standing there, usually trying to decide which decision to make, right or wrong? The person has his or her little conscience person standing on one shoulder and the little devil person standing on the other; each one telling him what to do.

Well, believe me! Since the devil temporarily won that day when I made my wrong decision, he had not ceased to tell me all the time in my thoughts for years afterward that I would never be forgiven for what I did no matter how many times I asked God, *if* I even believed that God was capable of forgiving me for what I felt was murder. Satan would tell me thoughts of belittlement, that I was worthless for my decision, in which case my self-esteem suffered.

When I was in my early twenties, an evangelist visited our town for a week. The Lord had been convicting me, and one night, while attending the evangelist's meeting, I could not stay in my seat any longer during the altar call. I went down front and asked Jesus into my heart as my personal Lord and Savior. I knew God was the only One who could forgive my sin and release me from my brokenness and shame.

Years afterward, God has placed on my heart the large number of pews filled with many, many people like myself . . . saved . . . forgiven . . . yet *not healed!* Maybe they haven't been able to believe or accept God's forgiveness and are repeatedly asking God to forgive them in case they forgot, or He did not hear them the first time, just as I did for years.

What a terrible feeling to live with! A voice in your head keeps telling you that *no one will forgive you for this, not even God, so don't bother asking Him. And maybe you already have asked Him, which is ok because He doesn't hear you anyway.* BUT, Satan (the devil) is a LIAR!

These people are all around us in our everyday walk of life. They are our co-workers, bosses, neighbors, friends, and relatives, passing us in the supermarket, talking to us on the phone, and vacationing and camping beside us.

People really should have God in their lives. They need healing from their guilt, pain, brokenness, and shame. A mentor friend of mine sings a beautiful song titled, *People Need the Lord*, by Greg Nelson and Phil McHugh. It is so true; if you listen to the lyrics. I can hear her angelic voice singing this song as I write this.

I encourage you to listen to the lyrics today and allow these words to convict your heart to accept Jesus and drive you to share Jesus with others. It's a beautiful, yet sobering, song. It reminds us how empty, broken, and painful their lives are. We can see and feel their hurt through Jesus' love. We have the answer. God calls us to shine His light into this dark world that seems to be getting darker by the minute.

In many cases, what used to be illegal is now legal and vice versa. We have the hope of the living Word from our Lord. His command is to share it and show His love to each other. Why is this so difficult for us to carry out?

God always has a plan if we just place our trust in Him. As I will mention in the next chapter, the theme we chose for our Continental's Mission Trip to the United Kingdom was "Mission of Hope" from Jeremiah 29:11. The New Living Translation reads: "'For I know the plans I have for you,' says the Lord. 'They are plans for good and not for disaster, to give you a future and a hope.'"

If you keep reading, it says, "'In those days when you pray, I will listen. If you look for me wholeheartedly, you will find me. I will be found by you,' says the Lord. 'I will end your captivity and restore your fortunes.'"

God has a plan for you, friend. Plans for good and not evil. Jesus is the only way. Seek Him. Let Him restore you, too.

No matter what brokenness you have in your life from past mistakes or decisions you have made, there is a God who loves you so much more than anyone can.

His name is Jesus. He has already died on the cross and risen from the grave to forgive you, if you will just run to Him, ask His forgiveness of your sin, and thank Him for His saving grace. He died in our place for your sins and mine.

Whatever your circumstances, past, or missteps— always hang onto hope. We have *an awesome God;* there is *nothing* He cannot forgive and *nothing* He cannot do!

In Revelation 22:13 (NLT) Jesus said, "I am the Alpha and the Omega, the First and the Last, the Beginning and the End."

John 1:1–5 (NLT) says, "In the beginning the Word already existed. The Word was with God, and the Word was God. He existed in the beginning with God. God created everything through him, and nothing was created except through Him. The Word gave life to everything that was created, and his life brought light to everyone. The light shines in the darkness, and the darkness can never extinguish it."

Genesis 1:1 (NLT) says, "In the beginning God created the heavens and the earth."

In John 5:39–40 (NLT), Jesus said, "You search the Scriptures because you think they give you eternal life. But the Scriptures point to me! Yet you refuse to come to me to receive this life."

Referring to Jesus' promise to return in 2 Peter 3:9 (NLT), the Bible says, "The Lord isn't really being slow about his promise, as some people think. No, he is being patient for your sake. He does not want anyone to be destroyed, but wants everyone to repent."

Psalms 116:5 (NLT) says, "How kind the Lord is! How good He is! So merciful, this God of ours!"

Psalms 68:19–20 (NLT) says, "Praise the Lord; praise God our savior! For each day, he carries us in His arms. Our God is a God who saves! The Sovereign Lord rescues us from death."

Romans 6:23 (NLT) says, "For the wages of sin is death, but the free gift of God is eternal life through Christ Jesus our Lord."

I invite you to pray this prayer aloud, as these words can transform your perspective, life, and eternal destiny.

"Lord Jesus, I know that I have sinned. I have made many poor choices, and I need a Savior. I am sorry for the way I lived. Please forgive me. When you went to the cross, I believe you went there for me and my sins. Thank you for loving me so much that you gave your only Son, Jesus, to die for my sins. I believe you died and rose from the dead. I trust you to save me right now. I surrender my life to you and ask you to come into my heart. Thank you for loving me and never giving up on me.

"Today, I know I am saved, born again, completely forgiven once and for all. I pray that you help lead me to live for you every day. Help me to find a Bible-believing church and read the bible daily, which is your living Word through which you speak to me to help me grow in my relationship with you. In Jesus's Name, I pray, Amen."

If you have prayed this prayer, I encourage you to seek out others you may know who call Jesus Lord and tell them of your decision.

I thought my salvation was the final answer to everything I had been through in my life, but to my surprise, it was only the first step . . . God had a plan.

A miracle of God was on the way. I didn't see it coming. I had no idea how detailed it would be, but I am thankful it came.

John's Story

John, on tour with us was a very jolly, middle-aged man who played the trumpet in the orchestra. While we were sightseeing one day, John shared his testimony. He told me he had gone on a Continental Ministries trip at age 16 and played the trumpet. This was before he had accepted the Lord Jesus as his Savior, but he loved playing the trumpet and wanted to go. He said that he had a great time.

That journey left a lasting impression on his life that he never forgot. Later, he asked Jesus to come into his heart and began to live his life for him.

Shortly before this tour, after he had signed up and been accepted, he was away and enjoyed relaxing in a hot tub. He had no broken skin areas on his body that he was aware of at the time. Despite this, he developed a staph infection, which quickly advanced into the bone in his leg.

The infection was not responding to the IV antibiotic treatment, and he was very ill. He said that he not only almost lost his leg, but he almost died!

As he stood there shaking his head, and chuckling, with his eyes wide open, still in disbelief, he told me it was a miracle he was still alive, let alone here on this trip.

CHAPTER 2

OVERCOMING OBSTACLES TO HEALING

Trust Issues

I was born a fighter, weighing two pounds, five ounces and dropping down to one pound, thirteen ounces. Before neonatal units existed, I was placed in an incubator with 100 percent oxygen since I was born thirteen weeks premature.

Later, in a study done in Germany, they discovered that this high oxygen level in incubators for newborn babies was causing blindness! God had another plan for my life, and my eyesight was spared! I was very nearsighted and wore glasses from the time I was two years old until I had cataract and RK surgery in my 50s.

I have always had trust issues in my life. I am unsure of the reason for my trust issues, but there are many possibilities. It may have been due to the abuse in my home life. My mom and dad did the best they could, but generations of alcoholism and dysfunction complicated my childhood.

My mother was an only child and had been raised by her aunts because her mother and stepfather were alcoholics. She never felt loved or that she had a family. Despite these issues, she attended college, obtained a master's degree, and became a high school English teacher and elementary school librarian. Because so many things had been out of her control, Mom was very strict and impossible to please.

One Christmas, when I was about six or eight years old, my sister and I received cute little school sweaters. You know how excited little children are at that age to open their Christmas gifts, especially toys and other presents. When Mom wanted us to try on the sweaters to see if they fit, we were naturally not overly enthused to do so right then, although we did like them. My mother returned them to the store, and we never saw them again.

Anytime we got below a "C" grade in our academic college prep courses in high school, which she insisted we enroll in, my sister and I were automatically grounded for the next six weeks until the next report card came out. Another time, my sister, two of our closest friends, and I walked down to the town library after school. The one girl's mother was going to take us home.

We got our communication with our mother mixed up somehow and didn't have her permission to be at the library. She came in to pick us up, angrily grabbed us by the hair, cracked our heads together in front of everyone there, including our friends, and we went out the door!

Another memory is when my mother sent me to town, at about age 12, with my dad to get something at the store. My dad was a great guy and a hard worker . . . and goooooood looking! Unfortunately, he was an alcoholic from a young age and wasn't around much while I was growing up or causing problems when he was drinking.

This particular trip to town ended up with a stop at the bar with me waiting in the car for Dad, as he said he would be out in a few minutes. I remember considering walking the approximate two miles home but decided to scratch that idea and sit out the wait. He was in there for quite some time.

I remember thinking years later that I sort of felt like a dog, as people take their dogs and make them wait on them in the car. I remember it was a nice day, no rain, not too hot or cold. When I told my mother years later, she said she probably figured he wouldn't stop at the bar if she sent me along with him. My memories of him are a muddled mess of abuse toward my mom and kindness toward me.

After high school, my parents said they would drive me down to the city, two hours away, and drop me off for my first day of medical laboratory technician school. They would find me a place to live while I was attending my first day and pick me up after school. The class was small, the teacher was great, and the schooling went well.

When Dad and Mom came to pick me up, Mom said, "Well, we have good and bad news. The good news is we found you a place to live. The bad news is they only speak Italian."

I rented a one-room efficiency on the second floor of a great, older Italian couple's home. I have to admit that again, I felt like a dog left on a doorstep as my parents left, and I cried myself to sleep, even though it was the start of the next chapter of my life.

Another time, when I was an adult and had children of my own, my mother told me that when she found out she was pregnant with me, she jumped up and down, hoping she would miscarry because she already had a baby at home that was four months old and had her hands full. She said she didn't want me then but was glad she had me now.

That was supposed to make me feel good, but I had underlying mixed feelings about what she said, even though I understood. She also told me that she always wanted to have a lot of children until she found out that my father was an alcoholic, which was a difficult life. That made her change her mind.

What my mother didn't know when she was jumping up and down because she didn't want two children thirteen months apart was that I would be born prematurely after only six months and three weeks gestation. Her two daughters would be ten and a half months apart. She said it was like having twins. She kept us corralled in a playpen so she didn't have to run after us in two different directions constantly. Therefore, we didn't run our baby fat off until we were older, so we were heavier to lift and carry. Mom, as a result, only weighed 80–100 pounds.

For my mom and dad's 50th wedding anniversary, my sister decided we must surprise them with a golden anniversary party. I was not too convinced, as my parents were not "happily married" often.

My sister wanted me to assemble a photo board with favorite photos from over the years. There were a couple of one-of-a-kind family member photos that were sentimental to me and did not have my parents in them that I hesitated to put on the board and take out of my house for some reason.

I added them to the board, and the party appeared to go well. Our parents were surprised. My parents ended up taking the board home from the party that night for whatever reason. and mom said she had it and would get it back to me.

When she returned the pictures, they had been removed from the board, were placed in a bag, and every picture, even the one-of-a-kind ones, were cut into pieces! I was shocked and hurt. Evidently, all of my mother's anger of being married to my alcoholic father for 50 years, and what she had to put up with, was taken out on my pictures. I just recently told my sister what had happened. She was shocked, too.

I could probably share many more stories, which when added up would contribute to trust issues. I do realize alcoholism is an addiction illness. To tell an alcoholic to just stop would be like telling me that I could never eat any chocolate again—only much worse!

I'm only half joking. I love and respect both my mom and dad dearly. I am sure they loved me too. They did a lot of things right in the midst of all the turmoil. They both have passed away now, and I miss them very much.

Dad's birthday was a couple days ago. He would be turning 95 this year. There are so many things I want to tell them, and they have at least one "miracle" great-grandson that they have yet to meet.

Proverbs 3:5 (NLT) says, "Trust in the Lord with all your heart; do not depend on your own understanding. Seek his will in all you do and he will show you which path to take."

Satan convinced me in my own understanding by paralyzing me with just plain fear of my mother to believe there was no other option but abortion. He convinced me without a shadow of a doubt that my strict mother would kill me. As I think back now, as an adult, 50 years later, and ask myself, "Would mom really have physically killed me?" My answer is, "Probably not."

In the summer of 2008, I was unexpectedly prompted by God through a Young Continental Singers group visiting our church to go on a Continental Ministry trip to the United Kingdom. I dragged my feet for five months, then finally applied, was accepted, but had to raise $5,000 in sponsorship.

As I just confessed, I have had trust issues all of my life, and this was a lesson in stepping out of my comfort zone and trusting God with everything including raising the $5,000 sponsorship money. As I reminded my husband that the $500.00 non-refundable down payment seemed like quite a lot of money to me if I was unable to raise the rest of the sponsorship, he told me that he knew the money would come in and I *would* be going.

I thought, *Lord, did you tell him and not me?* I told God, *If you want me to go, then you will provide the money by my birthday,* which was the end of April. One of my husband's co-workers, he barely knew her name, from another department walked up to him at work one day and told him that she heard that his wife was going on a mission trip and handed him a twenty-dollar bill! My sponsorship came in effortlessly by my deadline, and I was fully funded in three months.

The first day of rehearsal camp, I lost my voice. Still hoarse almost a week later, I remember asking God, *Why did you bring me halfway around the world to sing and allow me to lose my voice?*

Two testimonies were given during each daily concert. One day, while we were on our long bus trip to our concert, God gave me each and every thought of happenings in my life that were necessary to share my testimony. I thought, *God, you don't want me to give my testimony, do you?*

That night during rehearsal our director asked who would like to share their testimony. I said, "I will."

Has God ever **voluntold** you to do something you did not feel comfortable doing? When those words, "I will," popped out of my mouth, my insides did a little flip-flop, and I wanted to grab the words out of the air and stuff them back in my mouth where they belonged!

I thought I would go talk to the director and mention that abortion was part of my testimony, and he wouldn't want me to share it. He asked me how I was going to tie that into our theme of Mission of Hope. I had no idea what I was going to say next, but before I could get anything out of my mouth, he said, "Never mind, go ahead and share."

I said, "I didn't even get a chance to answer your question."

He replied, "That's ok, the Holy Spirit told me to let you go do what you need to do."

I was not off the hook! I would have to trust God with what to say. Psalm 81:10 (NIV) says, "I am the Lord your God, who brought you up out of Egypt. Open wide your mouth and I will fill it."

I had never shared with anyone what took place all those years ago and wasn't sure what I was going to say. I shared with a couple of the other women in our group, as we were lining up to go out on the platform to perform, that I had never shared my testimony before, was scared, didn't have much of a voice, and had no idea what I was going to say.

They prayed for me before we stepped foot on the platform. I had to let go and trust God to do the rest.

Deuteronomy 31:6 (NLT) says, "So be strong and courageous! Do not be afraid and do not panic before them. For the Lord your God will personally go ahead of you. He will neither fail you nor abandon you."

A year or so after returning from the UK, I had started writing a book about my testimony. We were at the beach one summer for a week's vacation, and I completed three chapters of the book while there.

Then I noticed that there was this fogginess in my left eye that didn't seem to be going away. I thought, *Boy! I must have gotten some facial moisturizer in my eye!*

After returning from the beach, it was still a noticeable problem, so I went to my eye doctor, who sent me to the eye surgeon to have surgery done on a partially detached retina. If I'd not had it corrected, it could have totally detached, very probably leaving me facing blindness.

Needless to say, I felt that it was an attack from the enemy. I made up my mind that there was *no way* that the enemy was going to stop what God had assigned me to do.

During the next couple of years, I had two more partially detached retinas, one in the same eye, and one in the other eye, again, all of which I had to have corrected by surgery that involved general anesthesia and keeping my head down for two weeks post-op until the gas bubble that they placed in my eye to hold the retina down flat dissipated.

Premature birth and cataract surgeries both increase the risk for retinal detachments. Praise God that He has provided doctors with the knowledge and skills to correct partially detached retinas!

I was fortunate also because the surgeon told me that in the one eye, he thought he was going to have to place a belt to keep the retina lying flat since it had partially detached before, but he told me after surgery that he did not have to do that. Praise The Lord!

A few years later, I went to a weekend Speak-Up Conference in Grand Rapids, Michigan, which was for Christians who were interested in learning to speak and write. I took the first part of the book with me and met and spoke with some editors. The classes I attended were very helpful.

I had called one editor before I went to the conference, and she said she would be there meeting with people for 15-minute sessions. I went to join my one small group, and there was an empty seat at the end. The lady who sat down to lead our group ended up being the editor that I had spoken to on the phone. One of the mornings when I went to breakfast, all of the tables were filled except one table with a seat left across from an unattended meal and a cup of coffee. I thought, *I have no idea who is sitting there. Do I really want to sit there?*

You've thought things like that before too, right? But since it was the only seat left, I thought, *Ok, here I go.* And guess who came over and sat down in that chair by that meal and cup of coffee? You got it. The same editor I had talked to on the phone before the conference, who had led the small group I was in.

God kept putting us together the whole conference. I did get to have a 15-minute session with her as well as others. She had heard the start of my book in our small group and told me she would be happy to publish my book at her company. All I had to do was finish writing it and get in touch with her when I was done.

As soon as I got back home from the conference, my mother was diagnosed and hospitalized with stage four acute mantel cell lymphoma. The physicians started chemotherapy treatments and the school where I worked started their school year the same week.

I had to call the editor and tell her that I would have to put finishing the book on hold because of my mother's illness. She was very nice, told me that she was so sorry and to get back in touch with her when I got the book done at a later time.

My mother fought cancer for four-and-a-half years. She did well at staying in her own home and keeping track of things before losing her battle to cancer. I mowed her yard, cleaned her house, helped with meals, and helped take her to her treatments and doctor visits as well as working full time. I miss her so much!

Cindy's Story

Cindy's mother had the courage to leave her marriage and take her children with her. Eventually, her mom met a great Christian man who married her and showed so much love by adopting Cindy and all of her siblings.

This fine man was diagnosed with cancer and became very ill. He would suffer with so much pain. He was so weak that he had to find alternative methods to treat his illness. Cindy's dad reached a point that he could no longer work; they lost everything. They were homeless. The only way that they got through this horrible time was praying and sticking together as a family.

They could see God work in so many ways. A family took care of them until they got a rental home. While Cindy was on tour and sharing this testimony, her father was cancer free and healthy.

Two days before she left for the mission tour, the family bought a house and were now out of the rental. Cindy loved God and gave him all of the glory.

CHAPTER 3

NOT KNOWING GOD'S VOICE

I wish I would have accepted Jesus into my heart as my Lord and Savior earlier in my life and had the Holy Spirit inside me to guide me by His still small voice. I also wish I would have been taught earlier that I can talk to God, through prayer and literally ask Him questions that He will actually answer if I listen for His quiet voice and/or watch for His guidance.

Did you know that He will answer? John 10:27 (NLT) Jesus says, "My sheep listen to my voice; I know them, and they follow me."

Often, He will answer in one of three ways: yes, no, or wait. But *how* do we hear God's voice?

God can speak to us in many different ways and sometimes chooses to do so just to confirm the answers He is giving us. He will open and close doors that only He can open and close, to get us to where He wants us to be or to stop us from going where He doesn't want us to go.

He speaks through the Bible, His "living" Word, which is a great reason to spend time with Him daily praying and studying His Word. The same scripture may say something different to you if you read it again the next day, the next week, month, or year because His Word is alive!

He may speak to us through someone we are talking to or listening to, which could be a neighbor, church family, friend, a pastor, or guest on your Christian TV or radio station who tells us what He wants us to know. We will know it is a word from Him.

He may speak to you loud and clear through your pastor or his message so much so that you feel that the message was just for you, like you were the only one in the room. It is exactly what you needed to hear or know.

I will never forget one day when I was talking on the phone with my Christian mentor friend. I was telling her about a life occurrence of mine that I was concerned about, and she asked me if I had talked to God about it and asked God what to do. I was speechless, which doesn't happen to me very often.

When I finally got some words together, I told her I did not know to ask God and that He would answer. She said, "You need to ask God and then listen. He will answer you."

WHHAAAT? Nowhere had I ever heard this before in my 30-some-year walk with my Lord. You can ask God things daily about your current life, problems, and needs, and He will answer you. I knew I could pray and talk to Him but was never taught to ask Him a question about any of my decisions or needs and then expect Him to answer.

It took me a while to *routinely* remember to *ask God* instead of hitting *panic mode*, which had usually been my first go-to!

One other day in a snowstorm in Pennsylvania, I was trying to back our big, raised-roof conversion van out of our garage, which had no door to keep the weather out. The freezing rain had entered the garage, frozen under the rear van tires, and I could not back the van out to go to work.

Well, I was starting to panic. I called my work and told them I would be late. My husband had already left for work, so I thought to call my mentor friend.

Do you think that was a thought from God? The first thing she said to me was, "Did you ask God about it yet?"

I just laughed and said, "Why no. I went to panic mode first like usual."

Then I hung up and asked God what to do. I put kitty litter under the rear tires, backed right out, and went to work. I worked for one of the best Christian dentists and the best co-workers in our area at the time. They sure never let me live it down that I was late because I was stuck in my garage—of all places.

When I started asking God first about things, and then listened, I learned He really does answer.

First Peter 5:7 (NIV) says, "Cast all your anxiety on him because he cares for you."

I don't know why I am still so awestruck by this. This is what it means to have a *relationship* with our Lord.

I really wonder if I had already accepted Jesus as my personal Lord and Savior, knew I could talk to God about *anything* and that He would actually *answer* me because of my relationship with Him, *if* I would have made the same poor decision. I wonder if I would have known not to lean on my own understanding no matter what lies the devil tried to tell me.

These are all rhetorical questions that I can only guess at answering. I would like to think that if I had been a Christian earlier, I would have made a different choice.

God gives each of us a free will, and we are all tempted in the flesh. We get to make our own choices, in our own timing, some of which could change our destiny, especially if we let it.

I think of Abraham and Sarah in the Old Testament book of Genesis 16. Sarah had not been able to bear children for Abraham. Leaning on her own understanding and timing, she gave Hagar, her Egyptian servant, to Abraham as a wife, to hopefully have a child through her, and Abraham agreed to her proposal.

But when Hagar knew she was pregnant she began to treat Sarah with contempt. When Sarah complained to Abraham, he told her Hagar was her servant and to deal with her as she saw fit. Sarah treated Hagar so harshly that she ran away.

The angel of the Lord told Hagar to return to her mistress and submit to her authority, and He would give her more descendants than she could count. The angel told her to name her son Ishmael, which means "God Hears," because God heard her cry of distress.

She was also warned that this son would be a wild man, like a wild donkey. He would be against everyone and everyone would be against him. He would be hostile against all of his family members. Hagar did as she was told and gave Abraham a son when he was eighty-six years old and Abraham named him Ishmael.

Then, in Genesis 17, God told Abraham that He would give him a son through Sarah, and he was to name him Isaac. The Lord appeared again to Abraham in Genesis 18 and told him that he would have a son through Sarah in the next year.

Both Abraham and Sarah had to chuckle in disbelief that they could have a child at such an old age. Satan probably was confirming these thoughts in their minds.

In Genesis 21 we read, "At age ninety, Sarah bore a son for Abraham who was 100 years old, as promised by the Lord, and they named him Isaac."

Sarah leaned on her own understanding, as we all do sometimes, and used her will to get what she wanted in her own timing, which caused strife and brokenness. She and Abraham did hear from the Lord, and then finally, in His timing, found that God not only kept His promise, but saw how truly awesome He is!

It may be helpful when tempted to ask yourself, "What would Jesus do?"

We need to discuss some of Satan's history and character from our Lord's view to better understand him and more about the Holy Spirit. Ezekiel 28:12–15, 17, 18 (NLT) talks about messages from the Lord saying, "You were the model of perfection, full of wisdom and exquisite in beauty. You were in Eden, the garden of God. Your clothing was adorned with every precious stone—red carnelian, pale-green peridot, white moonstone, blue-green beryl, onyx, green jasper, blue lapis lazuli, turquoise, and emerald—all beautifully crafted for you and set in the finest gold. They were given to you on the day you were created. I ordained and anointed you as the mighty angelic guardian. You had access to the holy mountain of God and walked among the stones of fire. You were blameless in all you did from the day you were created until the day evil was found in you. Your heart was filled with pride because of all your beauty. Your wisdom was corrupted by all your splendor. So, I threw you to the ground and exposed you to the curious gaze of kings. You defiled your sanctuaries with your many sins and your dishonest trade. . . . "

In John 8:44 (NLT), Jesus said, "For you are the children of your father the devil, and you love to do the evil things he does. He was a murderer from the beginning. He has always hated the truth, because there is no truth in him. When he lies it is consistent with his character; for he is a liar and the father of lies."

First Peter 5:8 (NLT) says, "Stay alert! Watch out for your great enemy, the devil. He prowls around like a roaring lion, looking for someone to devour."

In John 10:10 (NLT) Jesus said, "The thief's purpose is to steal, kill, and destroy. My purpose is to give them a rich and satisfying life."

Speaking of the Holy Spirit in John 16:8–11 (NLT) Jesus said, "And when he comes, he will convict the world of its sin, and of God's righteousness, and of the coming judgment. The world's sin is that it refuses to believe in me. Righteousness is available because I go to the Father, and you will see me no more. Judgment will come because the ruler of this world has already been judged."

In John 15:26-27 (NLT) Jesus said, "But I will send you the Advocate—the Spirit of truth. He will come to you from the Father and will testify all about me. And you must also testify about me because you have been with me from the beginning of my ministry."

In John 15:16,17 (NLT) Jesus said, "You didn't choose me. I chose you. I appointed you to go and produce lasting fruit, so that the Father will give you whatever you ask for, using my name. This is my command: Love each other."

Nancy's Story

Nancy was from California and was closer to my age. She said she was a hard nut to crack. She shared that she went to church, but when she went home, she left God at church on Sundays and Wednesdays and didn't take Him with her. He really wasn't a part of her life. She enjoyed going to church and memorizing prayers but never heard about how to make Jesus a part of her life.

During the last year of college, she married her high school sweetheart and later had two children. Fourteen years later, her husband decided that life was passing him by and made the decision to leave.

At that point, with an eight and ten-year-old, her life started to fall apart. By that time, she was ready to listen. God had been patient with her. He sent people into her life that shared about a God who could be personal to her, who loved and cared about her, and wanted to walk through this valley with her.

And she listened. She got down on her knees and asked Jesus to come into her heart, in the privacy of her bedroom. Nothing really happened except that she knew that Jesus really had a hold of her. She kept praying the prayer but nothing seemed to change. Then, one day, she decided to tell somebody. At that point, she knew that God became real to her.

Her children grew and went to college. Her son decided to start a band. They played in the area, had a following, then decided to make a record, and with a larger following decided to go on tour. He started to change.

Both children had accepted the Lord when she did, and she received comfort in this. When her son started college, she started praying for him because she saw that he was not choosing to follow God. She prayed that God would do what He needed to do to bring him back to Him.

While writing songs, the son thought that trying drugs would help him be more creative. In retrospect he told her that it was the worst decision he ever made. As she prayed, she knew that she had given him over to the Lord to do whatever He needed to. God did not answer her prayer in the way that she had hoped.

One day she received a phone call that no one ever wants to get, especially a mom. Her son, at 28 years of age, had died of an overdose. That was devastating to her. But because she had God in her life, she could turn to Him and ask, "Lord, why? I gave him to you. Didn't you care? Weren't you there? Aren't you real?"

In the middle of that night, the Lord woke her up; she went downstairs and began to write. About two hours later she had what turned out to be a love letter to her son, but it was God writing everything on the paper.

When she looked back, God had brought to her remembrance his entire life. They had been to Israel, and he had been baptized in the Jordan River. God reminded her of all the children her son had led to the

Lord while in elementary school. All of these things had led up to where he was.

The Lord told her that he was struggling, and He chose to end his struggle. And the prayer that she prayed for God to do whatever He needed to do to bring him back to Him was answered. God took him home.

She had God to lean on. She said she had hope because God had given her a reason for living. She knew that he was safe and that she would see him again. People would ask her how she could survive. She told them God gives her the grace to go on. God meets us at our point of need.

Whatever your need is, God is there to walk through it with you. In this world we will have trials and tribulation, but without Him it can devastate us. When we have Him to walk with us, we know that we have a future and a hope.

FEAR

The definition of fear in the dictionary is: an unpleasant emotion caused by the belief that someone is dangerous, likely to cause pain, or a threat.

That sounds more accurate than I would have guessed. Fear of my mother and telling her of my unplanned pregnancy was the absolute defining factor by far in making my decision.

Why was I afraid of my mother, who I am positive deep down loved me as only a mother could and should? My mother's upbringing and marriage was so abusive and broken that she never hugged us. When I would hug my mom, she would just stiffen up and not hug back.

From her reaction during these hugs, I could tell they were foreign to her, and she had not received many hugs—if any—while she was growing up or in her adult life. That was such a sad realization for me, but I kept giving her hugs.

My mother had a temper. I remember one time when I was about ten years old, my cousin, who was a couple years younger than I, came to sleep overnight at our house. We were sharing a full-size bed upstairs.

Of course, you know how sleepovers at that age go . . . there is much talking, laughing, giggling, and staying awake. My poor mother was studying for her college courses that night and kept telling us to go to sleep, but we were wide-awake.

I can relate to why she got so mad now since I am grown and have had to study for classes. Finally, Mom reached her last straw and came upstairs with her high-heeled shoe in her hand and began to repeatedly spank us with it through the thin covers. Let me tell you, that was no picnic! We did not say another peep even though we were still wide-awake.

But fear is not from God; it is a tool of the devil. Second Timothy 1:7 (NLT) says, "For God has not given us a spirit of fear and timidity, but of power, love, and self-discipline."

Isaiah 41:10 (NLT) says, "Don't be afraid, for I am with you. Don't be discouraged, for I am your God. I will strengthen you and help you. I will hold you up with my victorious right hand."

When I had applied to the Continental Singers Ministries group to go to the UK, I had to pay $500 down that was non-refundable before I knew that I would be able to raise my $5,000 sponsorship. I had to trust God to do it.

Then, after being "voluntold" by God to give my testimony, which I had never done before, at the last minute before going out on stage in England, I had to trust God to give me the courage and the words to say. That was one of the most difficult things I *ever* had to do. I not only had to trust God to be strong and courageous to stand up and share my testimony but also to bring it into the light, out of the darkness, so I finally could be convinced of my forgiveness and freedom. Christians need to do this to spread God's light into the darkness in our world.

When I was doing my testimony online for a Speaker's Bootcamp class years later, the audio part of the online app decided to quit. I had to stop and start that part over, as if I wasn't already nervous enough.

I remember one student had to chuckle, as she thought it was funny that I had lost my voice while on my trip giving my testimony and then again when I was speaking about it online for the class. When I videotaped my keynote talk at my church, I again was fighting laryngitis but it turned out ok, just like at the UK. God was with me once again. At the same time, I couldn't help but think that the enemy was trying to keep me quiet.

There were other times in my life when fear tried to grip me. Just after my husband, Denny, and I turned 41, he began complaining to me for about a week—which means he had that symptom for approximately a week before he told me—of something not feeling right in his chest. He thought maybe he had a rib that was out of place.

I told him, sort of jokingly, that maybe he should go to the doctor and get it checked, because it might be his heart. When he went to his family doctor, he did have a rib that was out of place, which the doctor put back into alignment.

Since my husband was never sick and therefore didn't go to the doctor often, the doctor wanted to listen to his heart while he was there. After listening, the doctor said that his heart valves sounded like an old, worn out washing machine, that the valves may be leaking, and sent him to have further testing done at a doctor's office in our area who dealt more with the heart.

This doctor found on the test that my husband's aortic heart valve was leaking profusely. He asked if Denny was having any symptoms such as blurred vision, swollen ankles, dizziness, or weakness on one side. My husband said that he was not.

Later we found out that aortic valve problems are asymptomatic. Denny was sent to a cardiologist in Pittsburgh, two hours away, for further testing. They discovered that day that his aortic valve was leaking so much it was messing up all of the other heart valves. His heart was working so hard to pump the blood back through his body that the left ventricle of his heart had enlarged almost to the point of no return to a normal, healthy, proficient, pumping size. When that happens, a person suffers from congestive heart failure—not much can be done to correct that condition.

We had just heard from a relative who was a nurse in Ohio, that there was a great team of heart surgeons in Pittsburgh. While we were at the office of the cardiologist, whose name was Dr. Joy, he told us that Denny would need a heart valve replacement surgery as soon as possible. Since we had driven such a distance to get there and were their last appointment of the day, they told us that they were going to scoot us across the hall to be seen by the heart surgeon that same day.

When we got there, we found out that we were in the office of that great team of heart surgeons that my nurse relative had told us about! They checked Denny out and scheduled him to have open-heart surgery two weeks later to have his heart valve replaced.

On the way home from these back-to-back appointments, we stopped to eat at a restaurant. We were both so shocked we could hardly speak. I am usually a woman of many words, but not at that meal. It was like we were in a dream that was not real. We did not feel like eating much but got some food down.

Within the next two weeks the real fear tried to set in. But God was working. I would lie next to my husband in bed, praying and weeping after he went to sleep. Praise God that Denny would fall asleep the minute his head hit the pillow.

We were both still working up to the day of surgery. He worked three swing shifts at the local glass plant, and I worked at our local dental office. We had two boys at the time, ages ten and thirteen. Our life was busy and I was not ready to be a young widow. But who is? It was a *HUGE* trust-God thing.

We went into the pharmacy for something, and an elderly man sitting there jovially started telling us that he had recently had a heart valve replaced! He looked as healthy as could be. We didn't know anyone who'd had a heart valve replaced because this was in 1996, and we figured it was a fairly new procedure.

On the day before the procedure, Denny, his mom, and I went down by the hospital to stay overnight. We checked in, as instructed, the next day, and physicians prepared Denny for surgery.

We kissed him goodbye, and then cried after they took him down to surgery. We went back to where we stayed and weren't there very long until the phone rang. It was the nurse telling me that his surgery was cancelled due to an immediate heart transplant surgery and where to meet him. We were stunned!

This was a Friday. When we saw the doctor, he said we could stay in the city for the weekend or go home. He gave us a choice to do surgery on that next Monday or reschedule it for a week or two later.

Denny said we were going home for the weekend but would return on Monday. So that's what we did. That extra wait certainly did not make it any easier! More fear kept trying to creep in. I had to capture every thought that was not from God, cast it out, and make it obedient to the Word of God. I had to pray and trust God.

Denny had to choose between a pig valve that would last about ten years, which would not require blood thinners, and a metal valve that would last 20 years to forever, but he would need to take blood thinners the rest of his life. He had a metal St. Jude's heart valve inserted because he did not ever want to have open-heart surgery again and had to take blood thinners because of the metal valve.

The surgeon told us after surgery that his aortic heart valve only had two flaps when a healthy one usually has three. He also said the flaps were almost completely disintegrated, causing basically an open pipe that the blood was washing through in both directions, messing up the other valves. We later found out that patients with two flaps instead of three have a much higher risk of aneurisms anywhere in their body. He came through the open-heart surgery with flying colors. I thanked God!

Denny returned home after a couple weeks or so and began walking around in the house, then out in the yard, then around the block as instructed by his surgeon. One day, while we were walking, we came across a neighbor man and his friend.

Denny told her that he just had his aortic heart valve replaced and where he had it done. This lady then told us that she had a St. Jude's metal heart valve replacing her aortic valve, done by the same team, in the same hospital, 14 years earlier.

We almost fell over! This was in our small rural town with a sparse population. Isn't God's timing just perfect and intricate? He put our neighbors, as well as us, on that walk that day for them to share that with us.

Seven years later, while doctors were checking Denny's heart valve with a yearly CAT scan, they found an aortic aneurism just where the blood leaves the heart and flows out into the aorta. He would need another open-heart surgery to repair the aneurism.

Oh no! He never wanted to go through a second open-heart surgery. That is one reason he chose the metal valve. Another trust-God thing. Did I mention this cardiologist's name was Dr. Gabriel, in the same group where we saw Dr. Joy? That was the name of one of God's angels. I took that as a sign from God to remind me that He was in control.

The heart surgeon gave Denny the option of replacing the metal valve with a pig valve, despite knowing that the heart valve was working well, to prevent him from having to continue taking blood thinners.

He chose to just repair the aneurism. Yet, another trust-God issue on the horizon. I began to pray and ask God for a successful surgery for Denny without any complications. They repaired his aneurism with a dacron polyester device that went up into his neck and curved back down, but it did not have the metal aortic heart valve attached to it, as his initial one was working fine. He came through it all again with flying colors. PRAISE GOD.

During these years we were raising two teenage boys; those of you who have done this know this is no easy task. By this time, our youngest boy was graduating from high school. Denny missed his graduation ceremony because he was still in the hospital getting his blood thinner regulated. I missed his graduation party that we had about a month or so later because of having to keep my head down from a partially detached retina.

God had protected our oldest son, Casey, and his friend when he rolled his car over at age 16, and many more times that I won't go into—and many times I'm sure I don't know about while he was growing up. He was enlisted in the Air Force for six years.

I prayed regularly for both of our boys, but much prayer went into our oldest one. I had to give him to God, lay him at the foot of His throne, and trust God to take care of him. It was not easy. God is so good!

A few years later, Denny got glass in his knee while working at the glass plant. Glass bottles were crashing off of the lehr next to him, shattering glass in all directions as he rushed over to help the man who was operating that lehr.

I was on my way home from the Pittsburgh hospital, where I'd visited my father, who had fallen and had a brain bleed, when Denny called to tell me he was on his way to our local hospital. We ended up at the same hospital again about a week later with a reddened cellulitis streak going up Denny's thigh. He could not have infection without being on an antibiotic because he had an artificial heart valve.

I was talking to God again about a successful surgery on Denny's knee. He had emergency surgery to get the glass out of his knee joint, without being taken off of the blood thinners. I had to cast out all fear. Another trust-God thing—one more reason to thank God.

A couple more years went by, and one day while Denny was hunting, he said his ear felt funny. He thought maybe it was from the wind blowing by his ear all day. Since he couldn't have any infection without being on an antibiotic, I insisted he get his ear checked for infection at his doctor's office.

His ear kept feeling funny and he kept going to get it checked. Finally, one day, right after he got it checked, the whole outside of his ear swelled up. It turned out that he had shingles in his ear for about two to three weeks by then. The shingles attacked his balance nerve on that side, and he could not walk and keep his balance well.

Because of Denny's balance problem, one foreman accused Denny of being drunk while at work. Denny told him he was not drunk. Denny is not a drinking man. That is another blessing from God after living with all the generational curses from the previous generations in my family.

He tried a therapy option, but that was not successful. The plant made him take off work. Denny ended up at an ear, nose, and throat specialist in Pittsburgh, who said that his balance nerve in that ear was still sputtering, and it would not let the other one in his other ear take over. He suggested administering a shot of an antibiotic into that ear, or letting neurosurgery go in and cut that balance nerve to shut it down so it would let the other side take over.

The ENT sent us to a neurologist who begged my husband not to do the neurosurgery because he would have to be off of his blood thinner and would be at great risk for having a stroke. I am a retired nurse and have worked with many stroke victims during my career, and I know all too well how debilitating it can be for these patients.

Denny told me he did not want to be like this for the rest of his life, and he *was* having the neurosurgery. I had to reject the fear and trust God again. I kept praying for Denny to make it through the surgery without any problems. God brought him through once more—blood thinners, heart valve, and all.

About two years ago, Denny finally decided it was time for a total knee replacement after all these years of old football injuries and scar tissue from those surgeries. He said he wouldn't miss his knee brace at all that he has worn for years while walking, working, and hunting.

We chose the best orthopedic surgeon around. Denny had to be off of his blood thinners for his surgery. I had to give him blood thinner injections while he got back on the blood thinner tablets and got regulated to his therapeutic dose. Another trust-God thing. Capture, cast out, and reject thoughts from the enemy. And *pray*.

He made it through surgery and was supposed to come home the same day. I talked the surgeon into keeping him overnight as a precaution. He came home the next day. I was giving the injections as directed.

On the fifth day home, he had internal bleeding issues from the nerve block given in the thigh pre-surgery, was light-headed, and passed out. He ended up with an ambulance ride to the hospital, getting a unit of blood and staying a couple of days.

The orthopedic surgeon checked him and his knee the day he was discharged from the hospital. This surgeon and his associate were both great through the whole thing. Denny recovered well. Praise the Lord!

We have received too many blessings to count. Do you think that Denny's rib being out of place was not a blessing in disguise? And what about bumping into those two people who had heart valve replacements and talking with them, before and after his heart valve surgery? The Lord wanted to confirm to us that He was in control and it would be ok. And what are the chances of having cardiologists whose names are Dr. Joy and Dr. Gabriel? Do you think finding the aneurism on the routine yearly CAT scan was an accident or a God wink?

God is always working for our good. Romans 8:28 (NLT) says, "And we know that God causes everything to work together for the good of those who love God and are called according to his purpose for them."

No matter what the enemy is telling us, God is not distant. He is close and cares about us and our circumstances. When we are going through tough times, or when we may not feel His presence, He is right there with us, lifting us up, and carrying us.

Mike Blackaby says it this way in the *Experiencing God, Knowing & Doing the Will of God* Bible study, Video Session 2, *Looking to God* (Henry Blackaby, Richard Blackaby, and Claude King, published by Lifeway Press, 2022) "God never takes us around our fears, He takes us through them. His miracle is waiting for us."

If we don't have God, who is our rock? Who do you run to and lean on when things get hard?

Some fears that the devil uses in his toolbox are:

Fear of what others may think.

Galatians 1:10 (NLT) "Obviously, I'm not trying to win the approval of people, but of God. If pleasing people were my goal, I would not be Christ's servant."

Proverbs 29:25 (NLT) "Fearing people is a dangerous trap, but trusting the Lord means safety."

Fear of what God thinks.

Psalm 118:6 (NLT) "The Lord is for me, so I will have no fear. What can mere people do to me?"

To hide secrets and things past in the dark and not bring them out into the light so God's healing can occur.

"When Jesus spoke again to the people he said, 'I am the light of the world. Whoever follows me will never walk in darkness, but will have the light of life.'" (John 8:12 NIV).

Fear of the future.

In John 14:27 (NLT), Jesus replied, "I am leaving you with a gift—peace of mind and heart. And the peace I give is a gift the world cannot give. So don't be troubled or afraid."

In Matthew 6:25–27 (NIV) Jesus said, "Therefore I tell you, do not worry about your life, what you will eat or drink; or about your body, what you will wear. Is not life more important than food, and the body more important than clothes? Look at the birds of the air; they do not sow or reap or store away in barns, and yet your heavenly Father feeds them. Are you not much more valuable than they? Who of you by worrying can add a single hour to his life?"

Second Timothy 1:7 (KJV) says, "For God hath not given us the spirit of fear; but of power, and of love, and of a sound mind."

Fear of the unknown.

Psalm 23:4 (NIV): "Even though I walk through the valley of the shadow of death, I will fear no evil, for you are with me; your rod and your staff, they comfort me."

First Peter 5:6,7 (NIV): "Humble yourselves, therefore, under God's mighty hand, that he may lift you up in due time. Cast all your anxiety on him because he cares for you."

THE DEVIL IS A LIAR!

In "The Meaning of Salvation: Wholeness Mark 5:24–34" by Ted Schroder (March 2, 2014) it is written—

"In the Gospel accounts of Jesus' miracles of healing, the word 'save' is most frequently used. The healing in these stories is always of the whole person. God's salvation concerns the whole person. Jesus' healing ministry is summarized: 'All who touched him were "saved" healed.'" (Mark 6:56, NIV)

"Jesus showed concern for the whole person. His compassion resulted in the alleviation of human need whether it was hunger or disease. He was seeking and saving all those who were subject to the forces of evil. He was concerned for the wholeness of the human personality. He is concerned for every part of us.

"The Greek word *sōzein* can mean both 'to heal' and 'to save.' The woman with the hemorrhage, a disease that made her ceremonially impure and increasingly weak physically has tried all the remedies she knew without success. She hears of Jesus; she comes to Jesus; she touches Jesus in simple faith that he can cure her, or that she could be 'saved' (Mark 5:28).

She went out into a new life of peace and wholeness. There was a complete and instantaneous righting of her relationship with God which comes about when she recognizes her need, hears of Jesus, and comes to him in simple trust.

"He said to her, 'Daughter, your faith has healed you. Go in peace and be freed from your suffering' (Mark 5:34). It explains in the study notes for Mark 5:34, 'The Greek word for "healed" actually means "saved." Here both physical healing "be freed from your suffering" and spiritual salvation "go in peace" are meant."

God doesn't just want to save us for a future with Him, but He also wants to set us free here and now! God is in control and holds the future.

Matt's Story

Matt was a great guy from Florida who played the guitar. He told his story just after Nancy's, on the same evening. He made the statement right off the bat that it was painful to listen to Nancy's story about her son because that should have been him from all the things he did in his life.

He told of growing up in a Christian home and being an altar boy, but had no relationship with God at all. He was playing church, knew Jesus was knocking, but would not open the door.

At 13 years old, he said he got baptized in a Methodist church. Later that afternoon he smoked his first marijuana joint.

It didn't take long for things to get a lot worse. At age 15, he was addicted to crack cocaine. He ended up spending six months in a residential treatment center. He was able to stay clean for quite some time. Life was looking up and he was doing quite well.

Christ was not a part of his life, so about a year later he started in a downward spiral worse than before. He dropped out of high school. He was able to get a job, which was good and bad, because now he could support his habits.

Matt met a woman who would later become his wife, and at age 23 he had his only child, which is usually a very special time. He did not take advantage of that being an awesome miracle in his life. His problems continued to get worse, and he became unbearable to his family.

One positive thing that did happen was that his wife's mother and grandmother were very godly women who would ultimately make a godly influence on his life. His wife started to drag him to church. As he went to church, seeds got planted, regardless of his trying to push them away. Luckily, they got stuck there. Matt was still struggling with things, but he knew that people were praying for him.

A couple of years after that, on the day after Valentine's Day, his wife and son packed up and left him because they had had enough. He was unbearable.

The next day was a Sunday, and he was sitting alone in his house, feeling as low as he could be. He received a phone call from his wife's mother who told him, "Matt, we forgive you; we love you, we want to be there for you, and we are praying for you."

He said it was like Jesus was talking to him. He hung up the phone after talking to her and right then, remembers dropping to the floor on his knees, sobbing, and that's when he opened that door and asked Jesus into his heart. He said that it was an amazing thing!

A couple hours later his wife came home and he told her what happened. His family really started to heal at that point, but not overnight, as it was a process.

That was 12 years before our tour date, and he told us that he had only missed church about five times since then—three of those times were while on this tour. He reminded the congregation that night that there is hope, because if God could save someone like him, as he was out there about as far away as he could get from Him, He could save them, too.

Matt pointed to the beautiful wooden cross on the stage and said that everyone would be invited at the end of the service to respond to the salvation message if they hadn't accepted Jesus into their hearts. He encouraged them to take part in that decision of hope for their lives.

(From left), All three grandkids: Dean, Brooks, and Guy.

CHAPTER 5

HEALING

One of the Continental team members came up to me after my testimony and asked me if I had ever named that precious little one. I said that I had not because I was not sure if it was a little boy or a little girl.

She told me to ask God and He would tell me.

I asked God, and I am not positive of His answer, although I really believe she is a little girl. I named her Cassandra, ("Cassie" for short). If he is a little boy, his name is Cory. I know I will be able to greet this precious one by name in heaven.

Isn't God so good to bring healing after so many decades of hiding and shame? Amazing! It's never too late for you to ask Jesus into your heart as your personal Lord and Savior. Cry out to Him for forgiveness from past sin, a choice you regret, and let Him heal your brokenness and despair.

I mentor this gal, Susie, who read my story in the book, *Anchor in the Storm*. She made the remark that I am both brave and healing. Susie said she cried the whole way through my story, as she had a similar story in her past, except she wanted to keep the baby and her boyfriend threatened her life if she did.

She said that she wondered if God ever forgave her for what she did, but now she *knows* that He has.

I asked her if she had ever named that little one so she could greet him or her when she gets to heaven. She said it was a little boy, and she was going to let God name him. Then when she spoke to me again, she told me what she decided to name him so she could greet him in heaven, by name.

God put another woman in my life who read my story and shared through tears that she had an abortion in her past. She had been in a very abusive marriage, had two young children, and was severely underweight and not physically well enough to carry and birth another child. She knew she would die if she tried to carry the child to term.

When I returned from the mission trip to the UK, I believed I was to share my story at my church. It was as if God took me half way around the world to practice with strangers so I could face my fears about telling my own family.

When I talked to my husband about the experiences I'd had in the UK and that I thought God was asking me to share my story more, he was super supportive and encouraging. I found *he* had stuffed all kinds of emotions such as pain, guilt, and shame deep down inside, too.

He told me that he had thought about telling our parents, but he thought that I would break up with him if he did, and he may never see the baby and me again.

Talking about the abortion and naming the baby together brought blessing from God in the form of more healing, through tears, for *both* of us that we didn't realize that we needed. That day I left the clinic and went on with my life as if everything was normal, I was quite pale for a few weeks and knew I needed physical healing. I had no idea I needed *spiritual* healing! But God knew! He knows what we need even when we don't!

Why does no one talk about the birth fathers and how this affects them? As I discovered, years later, by talking with my husband, he was deeply affected by my decision and still is, all of these years later. He still gets teary-eyed when we talk about it. I feel that many of these birth fathers are tremendously affected whether they know it or not, whether it is early on or has been many years, especially upon maturing as adults and possibly having a family later on in life.

I spoke with another friend who told me she had had two abortions in her young married life. She had been afraid of her mother, too! She shared feelings with me, which I found that I identified with, also that previously I did not know I had.

These feelings were toward our babies' fathers, as we wondered why they didn't share more of the responsibility with us when it came to the actual sexual temptation, possible abstinence, and birth control as it involves both parties. Why does it seem like the female is almost always burdened with the responsibility of these things, and/or it is seen as her fault, when both parties know the female is at risk of an unplanned pregnancy?

We had to deal with those feelings of unforgiveness to be totally emotionally healed.

I began to learn that there were so many different layers and levels to the healing process. As I mentioned previously, I had no idea that there was any healing necessary, except for the physical healing. Boy, I could not have been more wrong! The more years that passed, with my secret, whether in or out of the darkness, God kept revealing to me thoughts and feelings that needed His attention and gently, eventually, healed them, one by one. It is a process to lay it all at the feet of Jesus, and not pick it back up.

I have seen many changes in Denny as God has been healing his heart over the years. He has become much more outgoing and talkative. Often, I find myself waiting on him as he stands and has conversations with many friends, which is so different than he has been in the past. I was usually the one talking and he was waiting on me. My mother would always chuckle when the men in our lives did that. She would say that they were worse than an old lady, meaning that the older ladies are usually more talkative.

Denny has also grown so much spiritually over the years since I returned from the UK. He prays aloud at church and Bible study. He has always loved children, and they seem to be drawn to him. At church, our previous pastor's wife called him, "the kid magnet." He enjoyed helping her teach our youth group. *Who is this man?*

I have seen many changes in my life, also, before, and especially after, returning from my trip to the UK, as I told you about earlier. Our oldest son, Casey, settled down, and married a sweet girl named Meg. They are both great parents, and Casey is a great dad to their nine-year-old son, Guy, and seven-year-old son, Dean. We sure love these sweet grandboys. They are so much fun!

Unfortunately, Casey has struggled with back issues. He has had two back surgeries in four years to lessen pain in his back. He is still recovering from the most recent surgery, which involved inserting two metal bars and five screws to secure and hold everything together.

He is healing and it all takes time. While making the best of it, he hopefully will be healed and better than he has been in the past.

A few years later, our youngest son married a very nice girl, Brianna. They tried for a couple of years to have a child but to no avail. After each one got checked out it was determined that Buck had some physical issues since age 10, which he doctored for with a pediatric urologist then, but no one told us to follow up with check-ups for any reason, that all would be fine.

Well, 25 years later allowed a lot of time to pass without a good physical environment in which to have baby-making necessities. Buck was told he could have surgery but that it would probably not be profitable after so many years had passed. Brie, as we call her, was willing to adopt a child, if it came down to that, but Buck wanted to be able to look into his child's eyes and see himself.

Buck was upset, and doubted that they would be able to have their own child when he spoke to me on the phone one night. Even though my heart was breaking, I said that God gets to say. I told him that it may or may not be what he wanted to hear, but that God is in control and has the final word. I let him know that I would be praying for him and Brie.

I remember the day that Buck told us, as he walked though the front yard to his jeep, that the surgery was a success and that they would soon be permitted to try to have their family. I could tell that God got Buck's attention. I kept praying.

Buck and Brie then had two miscarriages within six months. They were crushed. I got to talk with Brie one day about my experience of being asked if I had ever named my little one so I could greet her or him in Heaven. I told her I named that tiny one whether a girl or boy and look forward to meeting that precious one by name when I get to Heaven.

She thought this was a beautiful idea, and I feel she may have done the same. I just kept praying. They then went to a fertility clinic, where a doctor said Brie was ovulating a bit late and that causes a much higher chance of a miscarriage. The doctor was going to treat her with medication, but before he got the chance to do so, she was pregnant again.

This healthy, miracle baby boy was carried to term and named Brooks. Praise God! Again, this time through the miracle of birth alone, I could witness that God was showing Himself to Buck and Brie and revealing what He could do through the long-awaited arrival of Brooks.

Isn't the birth of a newborn baby such an awesome miracle? It is just mind boggling to me. He will be 18 months old in three days, has his mother's blue eyes, complexion, and light hair, and his dad's silliness, sense of humor, and both of their laid-back personalities. What a joy!

Casey and Buck had accepted Jesus into their hearts as their personal Lord and Savior while they were children at church or church camp. Casey, Meg, and boys attend church. Buck and Brie do not at this time, but I keep praying that they will attend and bring Brooks up in a Bible-believing church. Proverbs 22:6 (KJV) says, "Train up a child in the way he should go:

and when he is old, he will not depart from it." Always keep praying for unsaved loved ones!

I know, too, that being a post-abortive couple has made both myself and Denny even better parents and grandparents than we would have been without that in our past, as we are even more appreciative of the miraculous blessing of children and are delighted to enjoy the many spectacular blessings of our grand-children. We certainly aren't perfect and have made mistakes, but it has been so awesome to watch God in motion over the years. GOD IS GOOD!

I knew I had to share my story with our family members, each at a God-designated time. My husband, Denny, and I sat down and told our sons, our parents, my sibling, and other family members that they have another little family member to meet when they get to heaven.

I didn't expect any comments from them but I'll never forget my mother's teary reply, "Well, you were working, so I don't know why you would do that."

My dad's comment was, "These things happen." I thought, *I never thought it would happen to me!*

My mother-in-law and sister-in-law cried and gave me a hug. My sweet father-in-law was already in heaven and had already met this precious grandchild before we got to tell him. Now Denny's mother has gone home to be with him and our Lord. We miss them both dearly.

The Holy Spirit ministered through me to my parents—which I never expected as my mother was a Jehovah's Witness—and I know that was completely a God thing! All of our family members received the news far better than we had ever dreamed. We were able to share a few tears together, allowing a closeness that we don't always feel. I thank God for that closeness.

The next thing I had to do was *forgive myself.* I had asked God's forgiveness for my past decision shortly after asking Jesus into my heart as my Lord and Savior, and at least a couple of more times after that, just in case I forgot or He didn't hear me the first time.

Donna

Donna was in our chorus and was from Arizona. She had a Quaker upbringing and had known the Lord all of her life. She still endured testing, trials, and blessings.

Donna was married at a young age and had three children right away. The Lord took her oldest daughter home to be with Him. She didn't question why because she already knew the reason. Donna's daughter was very ill, so in His mercy God took her home. Donna was grateful that she had no more suffering, though she missed her daughter a lot.

Donna's husband had cancer most of their married life, as four years into their marriage, he had been diagnosed with terminal cancer. He was a very determined man and dealt with it for 20 years. The Lord took him home four years before this tour.

Donna struggled with this, as it was the hardest thing she had faced in her life. She had always been a mother or a wife. All of her children were grown, married, and she had grandchildren. She couldn't understand how she could still feel so alone with all those loved ones around her and so many grandbabies crawling all over her. The Lord told her, *"Maybe you feel lonely but you are not alone. I am right here."*

Then it occurred to her that there had been so many times she had been so busy being a wife, mom, and serving Him that God took a back seat in her busyness. God's love was the most important thing. The love for her daughters and granddaughters was just the icing on the cake.

She was just settling into the single life and actually kind of enjoying it. She was getting used to it and felt it was wonderful, and the Lord perhaps decided she was getting too comfortable and brought someone into her life.

Two weeks before this tour he proposed. Hope for the future. God loves us. He knows the desires of our hearts and wants to grant them. God understands us deeper than we realize, she said at the end of her testimony, and there *is* hope for the future.

CHAPTER 6

WHAT IS FORGIVENESS?

The definition in *Webster's Dictionary* for the word forgiveness is: to pardon; to give up resentment of; to cease to feel resentment against.

As I matured in my faith over thirty years of following Christ, I **knew** *I had not* forgotten to ask Him; He had **heard** me the first time I asked for forgiveness, and my sins **were** forgiven by Jesus' shed blood on the cross, **once and for all,** because of His great *love* for me! I no longer had to *wonder* if I was forgiven.

Psalm 103:12 (NLT) says, "He has removed our sins as far from us as the east is from the west." Not only that, but He also *forgets* our sins. The Bible says in Hebrews 10:17 (NLT), "Then he says, 'I will never again remember their sins and lawless deeds.'"

In Jeremiah 31:34b (NLT), the Lord says, "And I will forgive their wickedness, and I will never again remember their sins."

He tells us that again in Hebrews 8:12 (NLT). Romans 4:7,8 (NIV) says, "Blessed are they whose transgressions are forgiven, whose sins are covered. Blessed is the man whose sin the Lord will never count against him."

Micah 7:18, 19 (NIV) says, "Who is a God like you, who pardons sin and forgives the transgression of the remnant of his inheritance? You do not stay angry forever but delight to show mercy. You will again have compassion on us; you will tread our sins underfoot and hurl all our iniquities into the depths of the sea."

When God takes away sin's guilt so it doesn't condemn us, Micah 7:18 (NIV) says He also takes away its power so it does not rule over us.

Psalm 19:13 (NIV) says, "Keep your servant also from willful sins; may they not rule over me. Then will I be blameless, innocent of great transgression."

Romans 8:1 (NLT) reminds us, "So now there is no condemnation for those who belong to Christ Jesus."

It really is a revelation! I finally was able to get it into my heart and mind that since the Lord of the universe, who is also my Maker, forgives me and forgets my sins, there is *absolutely* no reason for me to hang onto the guilt, shame, and pain of my past.

I was finally free, able to let it go, give it completely to Jesus, hang it on the cross, never to be picked up again, after all those years.

FREEDOM AT LAST.

Here are four principles from Dr. Richard Dorst's book *Journey To Freedom, 30 days to forgiveness and hope* (Ashland, Ohio: BookMasters, Inc., 2011, p. 48, 80, 100) to further support the healing of forgiveness and freedom.

- "Make allowance for each other's faults, and forgive anyone who offends you. Remember, the Lord forgave you, so you must forgive others."—Colossians 3:13 (NLT)
- "Forgiveness is a miracle. Through forgiveness what is broken is made whole again; what is soiled is made clean again." – Author unknown
- "The miracle of forgiveness doesn't deny what happened in the past, but it does prevent bad feelings from blocking the way to a new start. Forgiveness is seldom easy but it will take a huge weight off of your back!"
- "We've all been broken at some point. Forgiving ourselves or another person helps us move forward."—Academy Award-winning actress, Julia Roberts, quoted in *Guideposts*, January, 2011

Our church recently did a Bible study entitled *Soul Care, 7 Transformational Principles for a Healthy Soul*, which I highly recommend (available through Renewal

International). Dr. Rob Reimer, who created the study, shared this true story on the video in one of the lessons.

A lady came in to talk with him as he also counseled individuals. She began to cry and told him that she had had an abortion years earlier. She told him she remembers every little detail of that clinic clear down to the pattern on the wallpaper in the room and began describing it to him. She said that she was not able to get these things out of her head even after all these years.

After explaining to her that Jesus is always with us no matter where we are, he told her that he wanted her to close her eyes and go back to that day in that room and look to see if she could see Jesus in that room with her. As she sat there with her eyes closed after a few minutes she began sobbing profusely and did not stop for about 40 minutes.

When she finally was almost done crying, he asked her what she saw, and this is what she told him. She said that she saw Jesus carrying her son in His arms as He was walking toward the door. Jesus told her that He was not mad at her and neither was the child, He said, nodding toward her son. He said that when she gets to Heaven, she will get to meet him. She knew she was forgiven and would never again revisit that room with all of its details. That lesson really hit home for Denny and me.

Gene's Story

Gene, from Oklahoma, was one of the assistant directors for our tour. In 1983, he had accidentally driven a truck over a 300-foot cliff in Colorado when he was twenty-three years old. He had a head injury, which caused his head to swell up to the size of a basketball. His back was fractured, and one lung collapsed. One shoulder was destroyed, and he couldn't use his arm. He was facing imminent death. The doctor told his wife that he would be dead by the next day; to make funeral arrangements. However, in fifteen days, he walked out of that hospital!

The doctor said later that he had never seen a more broken body that was still alive. Gene also was told he would have limited arm motion, would only be capable of raising it to a certain height, and could never play the guitar again. On this tour he was playing the guitar.

God saved him for a reason, and for 45 years, he had been trying to justify his worthiness. He said he was not worthy. God's grace and mercy was his gift.

He said it was like his friend who was teaching his 18-month-old to swim. The friend told the baby to trust him. The baby would start thrashing around when he would let go. Then the parent reached out, held the child, and the baby calmly settled down. This is how we need to trust God, our Father.

CHAPTER 7

FREEDOM

Jesus forgives *all* sin. I want you all to stand to your feet if you *are* able, if you are not able, you may remain seated. If you are able and are not sure if you want to stand to your feet, do it anyway. I would like you to cross your hands and put them over your heart. Close your eyes. Take a slow deep breath and let it all out.

What brokenness, pain, or sin deep down inside do you have hidden away, that you don't want anyone to know about? Guess what? Jesus already knows. That thing that has been there for years, draining your spirit, holding you back from being the person that God wants you to be, can be released and forgiven, gone forever.

Very slowly slide your hands out to the sides and open your arms wide to give that "thing" to Jesus on the cross once and for all. Take another slow, deep, breath, let it out slowly and let go of that "thing."

Leave it there! Do not take it back! If you feel it trying to come back, do this exercise again, wherever you are, as often as you need to. Put your hands over your heart and close your eyes. Take a slow, deep, breath and let it all out. Slide those hands and arms out to each side and release that "thing" to Jesus on the cross over and over until it is gone for good.

The devil is a liar and sometimes tries to bring that thing back into your thoughts and tries to make you feel like it is still there. When he does this, say, "Oh no, no, devil! I have left it with Jesus on the cross, and it is gone. You have no place here! Be gone in the name of Jesus!"

Galatians 4:12 (NLT) says, "Dear brothers and sisters, I plead with you to live as I do in freedom from these things, for I have become like you Gentiles—free from those laws."

The definition in *Webster's Dictionary* of *free* is in part: Not imprisoned; not affected by a specific circumstance or condition; exempt . . . I feel that freedom is a gift from God. Its cost was Jesus's shed blood on the cross for us to be free from sin and death.

Our country was founded on godly principles by people who feared God. It has cost many service men and women their lives fighting for our country to protect the freedoms set forth by its founding fathers. Therefore, we should never take freedom for granted.

"Jesus said, 'If you hold to my teaching, you are really my disciples. Then you will know the truth, and the truth will set you free'" (John 8:31,32, NIV).

"Jesus replied, 'I tell you the truth, everyone who sins is a slave to sin. Now a slave has no permanent place in the family, but a son belongs to it forever. So if the Son sets you free, you will be free indeed'" (John 8:34–36, NIV).

Romans 6:14 (NLT) talks about freedom from sin's mastery: "Sin is no longer your master, for you no longer live under the requirements of the law. Instead, you live under the freedom of God's grace."

Romans 8:15 (NLT) says, "So you have not received a spirit that makes you fearful slaves. Instead, you received God's Spirit when he adopted you as his own children. Now we call him, 'Abba, Father.'"

The Bible talks about freedom in the Spirit in 2 Corinthians 3:17 (NIV): "Now the Lord is the Spirit, and where the Spirit of the Lord is, there is freedom."

Galatians 5:1 (NIV) says, "It is for freedom that Christ has set us free." Verse 13 (NIV) goes on to say, "You my brothers were called to be free."

Colossians 1:13 (NIV) talks about our freedom under authority, "For he has rescued us from the dominion of darkness and brought us into the kingdom of the Son he loves, in whom we have redemption, the forgiveness of sins."

I was attending a women's Bible study at our church last night. One of the women shared that God has been speaking to her about her past, clear back to her childhood—things she had totally forgotten—in order to break down walls that she didn't know she had even built up around herself.

There was a worship song that we sang a couple weeks earlier that God used to speak directly to her to break down that wall. She expressed that she had felt so much *freedom* since He did that and that He has continued to do more work in her during the weeks since. She could hardly believe that God could speak to her to break down a wall that she didn't know she had up for all these years and the amount of *freedom* that He would provide to her through it.

Some of the following thoughts are again derived from the book titled, *Journey to Freedom: 30 Days to Forgiveness and Hope* (Dorst 2019, 96, paraphrased).

"It is difficult to put into words the removal of the damaging, stifling, guilt-ridden, shameful, weight of brokenness and sin which has been like a super heavy weight that is finally lifted totally off of your shoulders forever by our God. It is exhilarating, fresh, new, almost hard to wrap your head around, and you are in awe of it all!

"Can God really be that good? He sure is! He says so in His Word. His promises are true. He keeps all of His promises! He wants us to be free from sin forever. Confess your past so that you can be freed from it. If you haven't yet entered into a personal relationship with Jesus Christ, now is a good time. Do not put it off until later.

"None of us know how much time we have left to live our lives on this earth. We are not guaranteed even the next five minutes. Ask Jesus to forgive your past sins, actions, and failing to do what you ought to have done and invite Him into your life as your personal Lord and Savior. Thank Him for His unconditional love and ask Him to help you to forgive yourself."

"You can't go back and change the beginning. But you can start where you are, and change the ending!" – C.S. Lewis (Dorst 2019,16)

Hope for the future is real for those who put their faith in God's gift of love, Jesus Christ. (Dorst 2019,102)

"Freedom in Christ is living free from fear, fully alive with joy and peace."—*Finding Freedom in Christ: A Study of Galatians*. (Roose 2021,110)

Susan's Story

Susan was raised in a Christian family, accepted the Lord into her life at age five years at a Methodist church's Vacation Bible School, (VBS). She understood Jesus to be real and understood that He was with her and her love for Him began to grow. She began to understand more about his being her Savior later in high school.

After high school, she married a man who grew up in a Christian family and became a leader in the church. They had two children and two grandchildren, including twin boys, age three-and-a-half.

Two years before tour, she had been helping her mother-in-law and returned home late at night. There was a note on the table saying her husband was gone but would come back in the morning and explain.

Susan looked frantically in the city but couldn't find him. He was her best friend. He came back in the morning and said that he had found someone else and was leaving her after thirty-six years of marriage. She was shocked and couldn't believe it because he had acted like a Christian all along.

They tried to work out differences for a couple of months, but he was so drawn to this person that he left. She was devastated! She explained that when you marry you become one, so when one is gone it's like half of you is torn away, which leaves an open wound.

All along her friends had shared scriptures, and one friend gave her a tin with the word "hope" on it, which she kept always before her. She had read Psalm 71, which God impressed upon her before she knew that her husband was leaving. The scripture reminded her that even though a person would see trouble, He would bring restoration. She clung to that because she felt God gave her that to minister to her.

She felt so alone. One day at her lowest point, as she was still grieving, she pulled a bottle of pills out of the cabinet and wondered how this would take her life. Her pain was so overwhelming she didn't think she could make it anymore.

But right away, God rushed in and reminded her that He would never leave her or forsake her, that He would never give her more than she could bear, that He would always be with her—Emmanuel, God with us.

She held onto that. She put the pills back; of course, she didn't really want to end her life. She hurt so much that she couldn't see anything else.

Four months after her husband left her, she was diagnosed with breast cancer. They caught it early so the stage was still zero. She had a lumpectomy then went through radiation treatment. They did see evidence of a micro-invasion, so they gave her a high 90s percentile cure rate. But she shared that we know that we don't live by percentages and that despite human estimations of life, Psalm 139 says that God has all of our days before even one of them comes to be. So, she trusts in Him. He has the number of her days ordered.

God used that, as awful as it was. Doctors had been watching something on a relative's mammogram but were going to wait to re-check it in six months. But when Susan was diagnosed with the same issue, they checked her immediately. It turned out to be negative, however, they found something cancerous hidden elsewhere and treated it early.

Susan received her radiation treatment from a robot. Her eyes were closed, the door was shut, and the lights were turned down low. She thought someone had entered the room, but when she looked in the direction where she thought she heard the person, no one was there. She looked all around, no one was there.

God ministered to her at that point by telling her that she was not alone. He was with her. Emmanuel—God with us. She finished the rest of her treatment and looks forward to the days trusting her Father, as she knows He is with her and will provide for her.

Things were not settled in her life yet, but then the first thing that came along that God said she should do was the Continental Tour, so she was there giving her testimony to give His hope to others.

CHAPTER 8

A STORY TO TELL

We all have a story to tell that will give hope to someone. I never thought I would travel halfway around the world, and lose my voice for the entire three weeks, just for God to open my mouth and show me that there are more ways to give hope and healing to the lost, hurting, and brokenhearted than just through song. It also includes sharing painful life experiences to say, "I understand and there is hope and forgiveness. His name is Jesus."

As I gave my testimony, I knew God was literally giving me the words to say, one sentence at a time. I could see God moving in the audience. A young girl in the front row had her head down the whole time I was speaking. I knew in my spirit that the Lord was at work in her heart.

After that concert, when I was walking back the aisle, before the overhead lights were turned on, an older gentleman stopped me and thanked me for sharing my story. I sensed that he also had something in his past that connected to my story. *You don't have to have had an abortion to know what it feels like to have made a choice you regret.*

I got to pray with a lady near the back (and her husband), who told me she had a similar experience when she was nineteen. Pregnant. Afraid of her mother, too! Scared. Stuck. Nowhere to turn.

Here we were, reminiscing about how each year we think about what age that child would be and what or who that child would look like. Our child would be 50 years old this year. She said she wanted to come forward to talk to me but feared people would know of her past if she approached me. So, when I came off the stage, walked to the back, and found my seat in the church pew beside her, we knew it was God. He knew just how to arrange our meeting!

I would like to share one final story.

Sally's Story

Sally was raised in a Christian home and asked Jesus into her heart at age 13. Sally quit high school to begin working. After a while, she met her husband-to-be, got married, and had children. Her husband was unfaithful, and sadly, their marriage ended in divorce. At one point, she was a single mom raising six children on her own.

Her doctor suggested that if she drank a glass of wine before bed, it may help her relax, which it did. She figured if one glass helped her relax, added glasses would help her to relax more. She became a "blackout" alcoholic—she would remain functioning but not know or remember anything she was doing.

One night, she laid down on the railroad tracks and went to sleep. She woke up in the police station. A train traveled those tracks every night at 9:20 p.m. But that particular night, the train had not come through.

She was also a smoker but was able to quit smoking.

She met another man some years later, and they got married. She and this man drove semi-truck together, delivering different loads of goods to various places. She found that he was an abusive alcoholic.

One night, while he was drinking heavily, he pointed a loaded rifle at her and threatened to kill her. By God's grace, he did not, and she was able to get the rifle from him as he dozed off. The police were involved, and she had them remove all of the firearms from their home.

One of her sons was in the military in California. They traveled to visit him from their home on the eastern side of the country, but ran out of money by the time that they got to Nashville, Tennessee. They decided that they would both find jobs to finance the rest of their trip. Sally's husband dropped her off for work one day and said that he would pick her up after her shift, but never came to get her when she was done working.

She was in her fifties, homeless for three days, and living on the streets with nowhere to go. She entered a restaurant and asked if she could do dishes for a meal in return, but the manager called her every name in the book and told her to get out of his restaurant.

She was sitting on some steps one day when she was approached by a couple of young men in their twenties who asked her if she had any place to go. She told them that she did not, and they told her to stick with them.

She traveled with them on foot around town for a few days. Sally said that if these guys would have harmed or killed her, it was a chance she would have to take because she had no place to go. They could have mugged, raped, or killed her, but instead, God sent these young guys to take care of her.

They were homeless, too, and showed her a pizza place that threw their left-over pizza from each day into the dumpster behind the shop. They knew what time it closed and all enjoyed a safe meal daily to keep from going hungry.

Three days later, she was walking down the street and met her husband walking toward her. She asked him where he had been, why he hadn't picked her up from work that night, and asked him where the car was.

He told her that he had to ditch the car because the police were after him. They had been living in the car, now it was gone, too, as well as all of their money, which he had spent on alcohol. Her husband ended up calling his mother who sent them $400 to get bus tickets back home. They never made it to California to visit her son.

Sally had fought for two years to get social security disability for her husband, as he suffered from liver failure from alcoholism. She just kept reapplying.

Finally, two days before his death, he received his first check. Then, when he died, they said they were going to take the check back. But after more review, they decided Sally could keep the check, which she used for his burial.

Sally met another man, and after dating a while, they decided to get married. During this marriage, Sally lost a son to alcoholism. She has two other grown sons who are struggling with the same addiction and one is not in good health.

The man she married was ok, but the devil was working overtime the last two years of their marriage, which were filled with quarrels. Sadly, he died unexpectedly at home while lifting an item that was heavier than his lifting restriction.

Even though Sally had accepted the Lord when she was a teenager, she did not have a relationship with Him until her third husband died. She explained that if she wouldn't have had her church family at the time she lost her son and husband, she would have never gotten through it. She is so glad she has a relationship with Jesus Christ and has her church family to support her and to share God's hope and love with her.

CONCLUSION

The enemy will throw all kinds of fear, lies, distractions, busyness, laryngitis, and/or problems in front of you to keep you from spreading the Gospel, telling your story, holding that neighborhood Bible study on your porch or in your area nursing home, teaching Sunday school, teaching youth group, visiting shut-ins, or whatever it is that you are trying to do to show God's love and heart and spread His Word of hope.

This is taken from *Ellicoll's Commentary for English Readers:* "The Christian Victory is a victory of dependence and of obedience, of dependence on Him without whom they can do nothing; and of obedience to Him: it is in keeping of His commandments there is great reward: and in bearing testimony that the testimony becomes a power and a treasure. So, it was the man who did Christ's commandments who was like the man whose house was founded on the rock."

Rev.12:11 (NLT) says, "And they defeated him, [the devil], by the blood of the Lamb and by their testimony. And they did not love their lives so much that they were afraid to die."

Read Joshua 1:9 (NLT): "This is my command—Be strong and courageous! Do not be afraid or discouraged. For the Lord your God is with you wherever you go."

Be strong and courageous! Our baggage, bad decisions, and brokenness are not too big for God's power and presence to guide us toward our life-changing breakthrough.

God does not want you to remain trapped in whatever prison of your past pain, or even one that you may be living in currently. I encourage you to pursue freedom in Christ. (See *Finding Freedom in Christ, A Study in Galatians* by Barb Roose, 133).

Trust God. He is good all the time. What a difference He makes in our lives. Having hope in Christ does change everything. Hope is on a mission, my friend. Blessings.

Dear Heavenly Father, thank You for Your promise to be with me wherever I go. When I am tempted to doubt and fear, help me to remember that You are with me. In light of this promise, may I choose to be strong and courageous no matter what I am facing. Thank you for being my Hope on a mission. In Jesus's name, amen.

RESOURCES

The Holy Bible

New International Version (NIV)
New Living Translation (NLT)

Helpful Websites

Unplanned Pregnancy
www.mypositiveoptions.org
www.knowyournextstep.com

Addictions

www.celebraterecovery.com
www.teenchallengeusa.org

Sexual Abuse

National Sexual Assault Hotline: 800.656.HOPE, (4673)

Inner Healing and Deliverance

Resources by Joyce Meyer:

Battlefield of the Mind: Winning the Battle in Your Mind

Change Your Words, Change Your Life: Understanding the Power of Every Word You Speak

Do Yourself a Favor...Forgive: Learn How to Take Control of Your Life Through Forgiveness

How to Hear from God: Learn to Hear His Voice and Make Right Decisions

Living Beyond Your Feelings: Controlling Emotions so They Don't Control You

Power Thoughts: 12 Strategies to Win the Battle of the Mind

The Secret Power of Speaking God's Word

Enjoying Everyday Life (TV Program)
www.joycemeyer.org

Resource by Christine Caine

Unashamed: Drop the baggage, Pick up your freedom, Fulfill your destiny

Resource by T. D. Jakes

Healing the Wounds of the Past

Resource by Ruth Graham (with Cindy Lambert)

Forgiving My Father, Forgiving Myself: An Invitation to the Miracle of Forgiveness

Resources by R.T. Kendall

Total Forgiveness, Revised and Updated- Includes New Testimonies of Changed Lives

Marriage and Family

Staying Power: Building a Stronger Marriage When Life Sends Its Worst
By Carol & Gene Kent and Cindy & David Lambert

ABOUT THE AUTHOR

Lynn Neely is a fighter, as she has survived what life has dealt her beginning with her early birth. She is a woman of bold courage and has a heart to help and heal others through introducing them to Jesus, His forgiveness, and the living Word of God.

Enduring a trying upbringing involving family abuse, generations of alcoholism, and dysfunction has

not changed her smile. Lynn has chosen to forgive—
including forgiving herself. She has also chosen to live
out her destiny that God has for her.

After enduring an abortion at age 19, and silently
suffering for 36 years from the gut-wrenching decision
she made, it is her prayer that no woman of any age,
or for any reason, will make the wrong choice that she
made at a young age.

Lynn, a national Christian speaker and author, told
her story in the anthology book *Anchor in the Storm,
Vol. 2,* so *all* individuals can know hope, forgiveness,
and healing from past choices they regret. Many have
not had an abortion, yet still know the pain of a decision in their past that they wish they could change.
There is *hope* and *forgiveness*!

Lynn is a retired nurse, paraeducator, wife, mother,
grandmother of three grandsons, and lives in northwest-
ern Pennsylvania with her husband, Denny. She enjoys
spending quality time with her family, going to church,
attending bible studies, singing, kayaking, going on
walks or rides through the countryside, and watching
beautiful sunsets and rainbows when she gets the chance.

Hope is on a mission, my friend. Thank you for reading my book. God Bless You!

To contact Lynn, visit her Website:
http://www.lynnneely.net
OR Email: lynn@lynnneely.net
            dlneely2000@gmail.com

Denny and me.

My parents, Ellen and Jim Amsler Jr.,
holding our first son, Casey.

Denny's parents, Bob and Violet Neely, holding our youngest son, Cody (Buck).

Buck and Casey.

(From top left), myself, Denny, Casey, Meg,
(From bottom left), Dean, (age 7), Guy, (age 9).

(From left), Brooks (age 19 months), Brie,
Buck, Denny, and me.

My sister, Brenda.

Made in the USA
Columbia, SC
20 January 2025

51271611R00074